FRAMED

I0139723

Y York

BROADWAY PLAY PUBLISHING INC
New York
www.broadwayplaypublishing.com
info@broadwayplaypublishing.com

FRAMED
© Copyright 2008 by Y York

Cover art by Michael Harada
First printing: December 2008
I S B N: 978-0-88145-406-2
Book design: Marie Donovan
Word processing: Microsoft Word
Typographic controls: Ventura Publisher
Typeface: Palatino
Printed and bound in the U S A

FRAMED premiered at the ARTS at Mark's Garage,
Honolulu, Hawaii, on 20 April 2007, presented by
Smashbox Productions (Tony Pisculli, Producer).
The cast and creative contributors were:

JOANIE .... Margaret Jones
NICK .... Keith Kashiwada
JAKE ....Jason Kanda
MAY .... Ginger Gohier

Director ....Mark Lutwak
Set design .... Mike Harada
Costume design ....Kathe James
Lighting design .... BullDog
Sound design .... Mark Lutwak & Kevin Chang
Stage manager .... Troy Apostol

Paintings by:
Jodi Endicott
Sabra Rae Feldstein
Margo Goodwill
Mike Harada
Paul Levitt
Meleanna Meyer
Aaron Padilla
Gary Pak
Tara Iden Spagnoli
Roy Venters

CHARACTERS & SETTING

MAY, *twenty-three*
JAKE, *twenty-eight*
NICK, *forty*
JOANIE, *forty-four*

In and around an American city, the present

Note: You never see their paintings.

for Mark

1

(*JOANIE and NICK's living room*)

(JOANIE *reads a magazine.* NICK *enters.*)

NICK: Love you. Don't wait up.

JOANIE: ...What is that?

NICK: What?

JOANIE: That shirt?

NICK: You don't like it?

JOANIE: I don't recognize it.

NICK: Yeah, it's new.

JOANIE: It's very orange.

NICK: It's bright.

JOANIE: That it is.

NICK: Peppy.

JOANIE: Do you mean "preppy"?

NICK: Peppy. It makes me look peppy.

JOANIE: Did the salesman say that?

NICK: No salesman. I picked it out myself. It looks peppy. After a long hard day at the office.

JOANIE: Where are you going that you require all that pep?

NICK: I'm gonna go meet the guys. You want to go?

JOANIE: Oh, please.

NICK: Come on, let's go. They like to see you.

JOANIE: Why?

NICK: I show up with my wife, they like that. Boss and his wife out on the town, stop to say hello to the employees—buy them a round or two. Shows respect; puts us on the same level. It's good for morale.

JOANIE: I wouldn't know what to wear.

NICK: I could pick something out.

JOANIE: I don't have anything peppy enough.

NICK: You don't have to be peppy. Just I have to be peppy.

JOANIE: What was I supposed to be doing while you were off entertaining your guys?

NICK: I just invited you.

JOANIE: You didn't invite me before. Before you were just leaving. "Don't wait up honey. Love you."

NICK: Gee, I thought I just invited you along. Huh.

JOANIE: No, really, Nick—how did you imagine me spending my evening?

NICK: I imagined you spending your evening wrapped up with your magazine.

JOANIE: I hate this magazine—

NICK: You always say that—

JOANIE: —an entire issue devoted to what isn't in a painting—who cares what isn't in a painting?

NICK: Let me cancel your subscription.

JOANIE: You will not cancel my subscription.

NICK: I'm going to get up early—sneak it out to the trash before you see it.

JOANIE: I need to stay informed.

NICK: You get in a bad mood every time.

JOANIE: I am not in a bad mood. I don't think you should spring it on me when you're going out with the guys is the only mood I'm in.

NICK: It feels a little bit like a bad mood in here.

JOANIE: No...no...it's just...if you're going to go to the trouble to get peppy, I don't think you should waste all that...pep...on the guys.

(Brief pause)

NICK: Where should I waste it?

JOANIE: You shouldn't waste it at all. Not when you see me all cozy here on the sofa. Waiting for you to join me. For a little visit.

NICK: A little visit? Right there on the sofa?

JOANIE: Right here on the sofa.

2

(Meanwhile. MAY *and* JAKE *in their bedroom)*

JAKE: Don't wear that.

MAY: It's nice.

JAKE: If you're my mother it's nice.

MAY: I like beige.

JAKE: You are not my mother.

MAY: It's elegant.

JAKE: Put on the red shiny one.

MAY: I'll be cold.

JAKE: So we'll call a taxi.

MAY: We will not call a taxi.

JAKE: Why not? We can call a taxi. Where is it?

MAY: In the wash.

JAKE: You haven't worn it—

MAY: How do you know?

JAKE: I remember when you wear it, it looks good on you.

MAY: Why are you so nervous, Jake?

JAKE: I'm not nervous. I want you to wear the red shirt is all I am.

MAY: I can't find it...I'll wear the black.

JAKE: What black?

MAY: Low cut. Peeking... (Gestures to her nipples) ...you know.

JAKE: Yeah, okay.

MAY: (Putting it on.) But if I slip out you shouldn't be surprised.

JAKE: Sit up straight it'll be fine.

MAY: I think it's too revealing—do you think it's too revealing?

JAKE: That's why guys look.

MAY: Who, Jake? Who is going to be looking?

JAKE: Never mind. Just be friendly, May.

MAY: Where are we going?

JAKE: The Lotus Bottom.

MAY: Jake! Why are we going there?! They don't even have food.

JAKE: Oh, jeez, May— *(Sigh)* I talked to some guys.
They said Nick goes there. Okay?

MAY: ...Oh.

JAKE: What "oh?"

MAY: I thought that was over.

JAKE: Nothing's over.

MAY: Did you get to talk to him yet?

JAKE: No, I didn't get to talk to him yet, that's why
we're going to The Lotus Bottom!

MAY: Jeez, I'm sorry—

JAKE: No, okay. Let's just go, okay?

MAY: I didn't mean—

JAKE: Okay, May. It's fine. We're going to go to
The Lotus Bottom and have a good time. We will
be smiling, happy, and convivial.

MAY: Con what?

JAKE: He likes happy people! With convivialityness.

MAY: You're doing good at the garage, you got that
raise.

JAKE: They don't appreciate me; I make them a
fortune—

MAY: I don't want you to be a laundry guy; they scare
me—

JAKE: I'm not going to be a laundry guy.

MAY: Those guys open the machines—it's like Vegas,
the quarters spilling out. One time the bag broke,
and I went to help pick up, and those guys, those guys,
Jake—

JAKE: I'm not going to be a laundry guy.

MAY: That's what Nick does. The laundries.

JAKE: You think a guy drives a new car every year from laundry quarters?

MAY: Maybe you could fix the machines—they're always broken.

JAKE: I will not be fixing washing machines when I go to work for Nick da Silva.

MAY: What will you be fixing?

JAKE: I won't be fixing anything.

MAY: You like fixing things.

JAKE: Come on, May. I'm a grease monkey. How attractive is that?

MAY: I could go back to the store. They said I could come back any time.

JAKE: You don't have to work.

MAY: I like to work.

JAKE: I'm making enough my wife can have her leisure.

MAY: I don't like my leisure.

JAKE: Get your hair done.

MAY: You don't like my hair?

JAKE: I love your hair. It's something to do. It's leisure-*ly*. It fills an afternoon.

MAY: I'm just suggesting...if I went back to the store, you wouldn't have to ask Nick—we'd have enough money.

JAKE: It's not the money, okay? Nick has a lot of class.

MAY: ...Then why does he go to The Lotus Bottom?

3

(JOANIE's *art studio; the next morning*)

(JOANIE *is painting.* NICK *enters with flowers.*)

NICK: Whoa. What is that?

JOANIE: Shut up.

NICK: Okaaaay. Bad time for a little visit, I guess...
I'll just leave these right here.

JOANIE: What? *(Sees flowers)* Oh, damn it. I'm sorry. Shit.
(She briefly stops painting to give him a kiss.) I love you.
You are not offended.

(She returns to slapping paint on her canvas. He watches.)

NICK: I don't get it.

JOANIE: "Your work isn't passionate enough, it isn't
violent enough, it's too literal and flat, it doesn't
reflect—." The fucking fuckness of the fuck.

NICK: What? ...What happened?

JOANIE: He sent back my paintings.

NICK: Who sent back what paintings?

JOANIE: Ted! Ted! You met him—the guy with the
gallery—at the benefit at the Hilton—

NICK: Which Hilton?

JOANIE: I don't know which—where you bought the
bottle of champagne for a thousand dollars.

NICK: Oh, yeah. I thought one of them cheapskate
C E Os would outbid me.

JOANIE: He was at our table, you said, "Oh, you
should see my wife's paintings." He said to send
him something so I did.

NICK: He sent them back?

JOANIE: "Dear Joan, thank you so much for sharing your paintings with me. F Y I: Artists usually send transparencies or digital images." ...I'm a complete laughing stock.

NICK: Which ones did you send?

JOANIE: The ones of the harbor.

NICK: I love those. They remind me of the pictures I grew up with. Full of adventure. They make me think about a world beyond our shores. The big ones, right?

JOANIE: The *huge* ones! Huge! I sent them overnight mail to his gallery.

NICK: You should put a gold frame on them.

JOANIE: Nick!

NICK: To make them look more important.

JOANIE: To make them look like they came out of your mother's house.

NICK: What's wrong with that?

JOANIE: Nobody uses frames. Particularly gold frames. The painting must become one with the wall.

NICK: Then what if you move, you supposed to take the wall with you?

JOANIE: God...can you imagine the laugh they had? "Look at this, boys, the boob sent her paintings instead of slides."

NICK: *(Deadly cold)* Nobody calls you a boob.

JOANIE: I'm such a fool—I'm a fool—

NICK: You want I should talk to him?

JOANIE: ...Don't you dare, don't you dare, Nick.

NICK: Talk—I said talk.

JOANIE: You do not need to resort—to resort to that.

NICK: I'm talking about talking, that's all I'm talking about...Now if I'd said "tear him a new asshole..." *(She smiles in spite of herself.)* But did I say that? I did not.

JOANIE: ...What do you think? What do you really think?

NICK: ...Sure is red.

JOANIE: For the passion. And the violence. It represents our passionate violent world.

NICK: What are you calling it?

JOANIE: *Landscape.*

NICK: ...Oh yeah, I can see that. The trees, the meadow, the sunset—sure. Landscape.

JOANIE: *(A smile)* It's an abstraction, Nick.

NICK: Silly me. All this time I thought it was a tree.

JOANIE: ...How do you tear a new asshole for someone who is a complete asshole already?

NICK: I would improvise. *(A hug)* I wish you wouldn't get so upset. What does he know?

JOANIE: A lot, Nick. He knows a lot. He has a gallery.

NICK: He's one guy. People like your pictures—people buy them—

JOANIE: Not recently.

NICK: Last week.

JOANIE: The week before last. I want him to like what I do. I want him to put me in his gallery. I want a show.

NICK: You have a show.

JOANIE: A bunch of artists at a high school cafeteria is not a show. It's a joke.

NICK: No, it's an honor. You should put in the harbor ones.

JOANIE: Nick! What if Ted comes? I can't put in paintings he already rejected. This one. I'm going to show this one.

NICK: Oh. Okay. Yeah, it's good. I particularly like the trees—

JOANIE: This is going to stop being funny very soon.

NICK: Did you invite him to the opening?

JOANIE: I mailed him an invitation.

NICK: Then we'll hear what "Ted" has to say about Landscape at the opening.

JOANIE: Right, he's got nowhere better to go on a Friday night than an art show at a high school.

NICK: When you're in the show, there is nowhere better to go.

4

(Later. The art studio)

(MAY with her canvas approaches JOANIE as JOANIE paints at her easel.)

MAY: Excuse me, Mrs Silver...

JOANIE: That's Ms Silver.

MAY: Oh. Sorry. Um...I was wondering...will we learn to draw faces?

JOANIE: You get faces in the second month.

MAY: But I don't want to learn tree anatomy.

JOANIE: It's not really anatomy—anatomy was just a metaphor—

MAY: I want to learn a face.

JOANIE: And you will. Meanwhile you will paint a tree. A leaf. You can't do a face until you learn musculature.

MAY: "Musculature" might take too long.

JOANIE: I have a pedagogy...a list...a list of what I teach in the order I teach it, and I promise you faces are on the list. Believe me, painting a leaf is preparation for painting a cheek.

MAY: Okay, so you intend to teach me faces someday, but what if I'm not here that day?

JOANIE: Every Thursday for three months—

MAY: I know and I'll try to come—

JOANIE: No, you can't miss—

MAY: Look, I paid my money—

JOANIE: It's more than money. If you're not willing to come to class, how willing will you be to invest the time needed for you to grow and learn? Art takes a lifetime. All I'm asking is once a week for three months. Didn't you know that when you signed up?

MAY: I knew it, I know it, see, I got the flyer. *(She shows a crumpled flyer.)* Three months, it says so right here.

JOANIE: Where did you get that?

MAY: The message board at the laundry—

JOANIE: Why did you take it down?

MAY: So I had the address—

JOANIE: You're supposed to take one of these—then leave the flyer so that other people can know about the class.

MAY: You want me to put it back?

JOANIE: Never mind. It's three months. Faces in Month Two.

MAY: Yeah, and maybe I'll be here every single time, but on the other hand, maybe I won't be able to make it, then I won't have learned faces and faces is why I'm here.

(JOANIE *focuses on* MAY, *which makes* MAY *nervous.*)

JOANIE: ...Why wouldn't you be able to make it?

MAY: Well...I might get sick...or I might...get sick or something. And I really want to learn how to do a face before I can't come...due to illness.

JOANIE: ...Let me see your tree. *(Takes canvas)* This is not a tree.

MAY: I did this instead.

JOANIE: You aren't supposed to do things instead. You are supposed to copy my example. What is it? *(Turning it around.)* A housing project?

MAY: *(Turning it right side up)* It's housing...and it's a face. Here, a profile.

JOANIE: Oh.

MAY: Do you see it?

JOANIE: I do. *(Slightly awed)* It's housing. It's a face. Housing. Face. *(Brief pause)* Very interesting indeed. But first you will paint the tree. The face is in two months.

MAY: I don't think I can wait. Maybe I should look for another teacher.

(MAY *tries to take her painting back, but* JOANIE *hangs on to it.*)

JOANIE: Now now, of course you can wait. What was your name, dear?

MAY: My name was May. *May.* That's what the "M"
is for at the bottom of the picture. See? I learned
something already. You painted a "J" at the bottom of
your picture, so I painted an "M" at the bottom of mine.
I didn't paint May.

JOANIE: What kind of face are you interested in
learning?

MAY: Female. Late thirties. Brunette. Heavy set.

JOANIE: That sounds pretty specific.

MAY: Yeah, it's a lady. I want to paint her.

JOANIE: Do you have a photograph of her?

MAY: I don't. See, that's the point. I don't have a
photograph. But I can remember what she looks like
and I need to learn how to paint before I forget. So I
can have a picture.

JOANIE: Is she...

MAY: What?

JOANIE: Is she dead?

MAY: Of course she's dead! Jeez. What are you—?
Homeland security?

JOANIE: Well....May...What if I show you a few pointers,
you practice them, and you come by, say before class
and we go over your work.

MAY: You're going to let me do faces?

JOANIE: Yes. But you still have to practice the trees
in class. Trees will make your faces better. Faces you
practice at home.

MAY: I can't do anything at home. Everything I do,
I have to do here.

JOANIE: You can take some supplies—

MAY: No. I'll practice here. I'm not going to practice at home.

5

(*Later.* JAKE *outside of a church*)

(MAY *enters.*)

JAKE: Hey—I was worried.

MAY: Oh, I was—

JAKE: Did you forget?

MAY: I didn't forget. I'm here, aren't I?

JAKE: I called.

MAY: I had it turned off...I was at Curves.

JAKE: Yeah? Working out?

MAY: Yeah. I just forgot about the time is all.

JAKE: See, I knew you'd like it. What's on your hands?

MAY: ...They were...painting—the walls—

JAKE: Wow, a lot of colors—

MAY: Did you go in yet?

JAKE: I can't go in church without you.

MAY: No, go ahead.

JAKE: I don't know what to say to him.

MAY: Tell him you want to convert.

JAKE: That's all?

MAY: Sure. He'll throw some holy water on you and bingo!

JAKE: Don't I have to read something and promise?

MAY: I don't know. Everybody I know was born into it and half of them are really sorry. Look, do you see a line out here, people trying to get in? There's only a line of people trying to get out.

JAKE: Don't you want us to get married?

MAY: We're already married.

JAKE: In the church.

MAY: No.

JAKE: Why not?

MAY: I don't want to go to confession.

JAKE: We'll both go.

MAY: You have to tell him everything.

JAKE: So we'll tell him.

MAY: Everything. Bedroom things. I can't tell that stuff to some guy who isn't even married.

JAKE: Can't you just lump it all together, "Oh, and a few other things I can't think of right now."

MAY: *You* confess. You can blame the bedroom sins on me. "My wife makes me pull out, Father."

JAKE: That's a sin?

MAY: It's a sin to spill it on the ground. Like littering.

JAKE: You said we're not ready for kids.

MAY: And if you're not ready for kids you're not supposed to do it.

JAKE: ...I thought this would make you happy.

MAY: If this is for me I want to go home.

JAKE: What do you mean if it's for you? Who else is it for?

MAY: *(Brief pause.)* I think it's for somebody else.

JAKE: Who else is there?

MAY: You. There's you.

JAKE: ...Well, I've been thinking a lot...about stuff... and...God and all...and it wouldn't hurt...to go to church.

MAY: You've been thinking about God?

JAKE: Yeah, a little.

MAY: When?

JAKE: I don't know.

MAY: Because you weren't thinking about God last night—

JAKE: Hey, hey—I don't like to talk about that stuff.

MAY: Were you thinking about God when you boosted that exhaust system?

JAKE: They owe me—

MAY: Yeah? God say that? "Thou shalt steal an exhaust system, Jake."

JAKE: May—see? All these terrible things I do. I need to convert so I can be more holy. *(She sighs.)* What?

MAY: You want to be seen in there. You want Nick to see you get a wafer.

6

(Meanwhile, JOANIE *in her living room, looking at* MAY's *painting.*

(Enter NICK, *who kisses her cheek.)*

NICK: Whoa. That is amazing.

JOANIE: You think so?

NICK: A real break-through.

JOANIE: Why?

NICK: It's everything you said you wanted—emotion over...what was it?

JOANIE: Technique.

NICK: Yeah, emotion over technique. That's a pretty emotional face.

JOANIE: ...You see the face?

NICK: Here. Crummy high-rise. Profile. Trapped. Very emotional.

JOANIE: Yes?

NICK: Isn't that what you intended?

JOANIE: You are a terrible art critic.

NICK: That's because I don't have the ascot—

JOANIE: She's a beginner, Nick, an absolute beginner.

NICK: It's not yours?

JOANIE: It's a new student. She has something, but she has absolutely no technique, none, it's amazing you can see the face, she's guessing at everything she does. You should see her, she's a little slut shirt, but she is desperate to learn. She's sneaking the classes.

NICK: Sneaking from who?

JOANIE: Some husband, boyfriend, I don't know. That's why I've got her picture. She can't take it home.

NICK: She said that?

JOANIE: She said it doesn't go with her sofa.

NICK: Maybe it doesn't go with her sofa.

JOANIE: Nick, please.

NICK: You don't bring things home that don't go with our sofa.

JOANIE: I'm telling you, it's some husband thing.

NICK: Who is she?

JOANIE: May somebody. Little May from the Hood. Hiding her art. Terrified that the world will mock her pathetic attempts to paint. Married to some knucklehead who doesn't appreciate her being an artist.

NICK: Like you are?

JOANIE: I'm not— I am not married to a knucklehead, thank you very much.

NICK: What are you going to do with it?

JOANIE: Put it up, study it. Figure out how I can help her, mentor her, what she needs to grow. My protegé. *(Giggles with pleasure.)*

NICK: Put it up here?

JOANIE: Why not? ...You said you like it.

NICK: Well...sure—

JOANIE: You said "whoa" if I recall. ...What? You were pretending?

NICK: *(Caught.)* No, it's good. I like it. Just...if I have a choice between looking at a painting of yours and a painting of your student's, I take a painting of yours.

JOANIE: You thought it was mine so you said it was good.

NICK: Joanie, I really like it—

JOANIE: You are so busted. I can never trust you to tell me a painting is good or not.

NICK: You can trust me, I would never lie to you. The painting is good, but it completely lacks technique, that's what I thought when I saw it, "Joanie is abandoning her technique to explore her emotions." The painting has no technique—

JOANIE: None.

NICK: Absolutely none. But it's good. For what it is.

JOANIE: If I can't trust you, it is just, it is hopeless, Nick.

NICK: But you can, so it's not. Nothing's hopeless here, it's all hopeful. You got your students, you got the restaurant, you got your show.

JOANIE: My show. *(Tisks)*

NICK: It's going to be great.

JOANIE: With homemade cookies and fruit punch.

NICK: You want champagne—? Dom Perignon—

JOANIE: It's a school, Nick. You can't have alcohol.

NICK: People don't need alcohol, they got art.

JOANIE: What's he going to think? Cookies.

NICK: Who?

JOANIE: Ted.

NICK: Teeeed. Whadayouknow. Ted is coming. There, you see?

JOANIE: He R S V Pd. What am I going to say to him?

NICK: "Good evening, Ted, nice ascot."

JOANIE: I didn't understand a thing he said about the Harbor pictures. "Blur the lines, Joan, blur them." What lines was he talking about? I'm teaching my students how to outline a leaf and he's saying "the ship *is* the sky."...

NICK: Don't say anything at all. Be silent, be mysterious. He's the ones with all the words. Let him define *Landscape.*

JOANIE: As what, crap?

NICK: As the next new thing. Isn't that what these guys are always looking for? The next new thing?

JOANIE: You think I'm the next new thing?

NICK: Ms. Joan Silver. The next new thing.

7

(The next night. The art show)

(JAKE and MAY look at a painting, it mystifies them slightly. Then:)

MAY: I want to leave.

JAKE: What is the matter with you? We are not leaving.

MAY: What are you up to?

JAKE: What are you talking about?

MAY: I'm talking about why did you bring me to an art show?

JAKE: We can go to an art show as much as anybody.

MAY: But we don't.

JAKE: We are today. What's the big deal? It's for anybody.

MAY: Have you been talking to somebody?

JAKE: *(Guilty)* What do you mean? I haven't been talking to anybody. What do you mean?

MAY: I don't know what I mean, I mean we've never been to an art show ever, and all of a sudden we're at an art show.

JAKE: Okay, okay. Calm down. Nick. Nick's going to be here.

MAY: ...Nick's going to be here?

JAKE: That's what I said.

MAY: Oh. *(Brief pause. She calms down.)* Okay. Nick. We're looking for Nick da Silva.

JAKE: That's right.

MAY: So, it's not about the art or anything.

JAKE: Jeez, no.

MAY: Okay. *(Brief pause)* Aren't you sick of chasing him around and never finding him?

JAKE: I'm not chasing.

MAY: *You* wait for Nick. I'm going to go.

JAKE: You're not going to go.

MAY: I'm freezing. Do you see this? *(Her nipples)* They're poking so hard they hurt.

JAKE: Yeah, you look hot.

MAY: Are you dangling me? Are you dangling me like some kind of bait? I am not bait.

JAKE: No, but you are as pretty as a picture.

MAY: *(Sees her painting)* Oh my god.

JAKE: What—what's wrong?

MAY: Nothing.

JAKE: *(Looking)* What is it? An apartment house? I think it's supposed to be a dumpy apartment house.

(Enter JOANIE.)

JOANIE: Hi. Listen, I can explain about your painting—

MAY: How do you do? Are you the artist? The artist of this picture? What does the "M" stand for—? Is that your name, *M*? Or is it some art name, not your real

name, but your artist name you put on paintings
so nobody knows who you are?

JAKE: *(He is astonished.)* May. Chill, okay?

JOANIE: *(Carefully)* Yes. I'm the artist. "M" is my art
name. For this painting. Because...because it's a new
genre for me. Usually I just sign with a "J" which is
for Joan. This one is mine, too. Signed with a "J".

JAKE: Oh yeah, I like red. I mean I like the "M" one, too,
but I like the red one. But that one is good, too, the "M"
one.

JOANIE: The "M" one represents a new genre. I'm
experimenting.

JAKE: Uh huh. What's the "M" stand for?

JOANIE: Mystery. How do you do. I'm Joan Silver.

JAKE: Hi. Jake Carter. And this is my wife, May.

JOANIE: Pleasure.

MAY: Uh huh. Me, too.

(Enter NICK.*)*

NICK: Look at that. It looks great, Joanie.

JOANIE: What are you doing here?

JAKE: Nick!

NICK: *(To* JAKE*)* What?

JAKE: Hi. Uh. Hi. Jake. I'm Jake. *(Brief pause)* I worked
on your Titan. Lee Automotive.

NICK: Oh. Hey.

JOANIE: I thought you weren't coming.

NICK: I couldn't miss your opening. And who is this?

JOANIE: This is May. This is Nick.

NICK: You're the art student?

MAY/JOANIE: No.

(NICK *looks at* MAY's *painting, then at* JOANIE; *he says no more about it. Actively.*)

JAKE: *(Blurts into the silence.)* We really love art. Isn't that right, May?

JOANIE: *(Pointedly.)* May and Jake are art patrons. Looking at art. I was just explaining how I paint in two personas. The "J" and the "M". This is my "M" persona. This is my "J"....And that's all of the explanation I feel comfortable with right now. Okay?

MAY: ...You know, Mrs—Uh—Ms Silver—? ...I saw a picture down there, down that hall, and I need someone to explain it to me.

JAKE: May—

JOANIE: I'll try. Far be it from me to explain some other artist's work, but let's go look at it. You two don't mind?

NICK: We're fine. Right, Jake?

JAKE: Great.

JOANIE: Let's go take a look.

(JOANIE *and* MAY *exit.*)

JAKE: You girls have a good time.

NICK: *(He is amused but careful.)* So. You're an art patron.

JAKE: Oh, I love pictures. We love both of these, the "M" one and the "J" one.

NICK: Ah, yes.

JAKE: What do you call that one? The "J" one.

NICK: The red one?

JAKE: Ah. "The Red One."

NICK: ...No. She doesn't *call it* the red one. It *is* the red one. I think she calls it *Landscape.*

JAKE: We love it. We love the red.

NICK: Well, you're too late.

JAKE: Too late for what?

NICK: To buy it. *(He puts a sticker on the card next to the painting.)*

JAKE: What's that?

NICK: It's a little sticker to tell everybody that this painting is sold.

JAKE: *(Reads the card)* Two grand?

NICK: Two grand.

JAKE: And somebody paid that?

NICK: The husband of the artist.

JAKE: Poor guy.

NICK: Jake. I'm the husband of the artist—me—

JAKE: Oh.

NICK: Yes. She doesn't know of course.

JAKE: That you're her husband? Ha-a.

NICK: That I bought it. And no one should tell her, either. Are we very clear about that?

JAKE: Oh, no—I wouldn't—but it's nice you bought it. Two grand. If it was me, I'd tell her.

NICK: No. She must think it's going into the great commercial void.

JAKE: Why?

NICK: Because a husband's purchase has no value. Whereas a stranger's purchase has great value.

JAKE: Where are you going to hide it?

NICK: Over my desk at the office.

JAKE: She'll see it.

NICK: She doesn't go to my office.

JAKE: Oh. Well. Maybe I could...buy the "M" one.

NICK: You buy the "M" one? *(Greatly amused at this)* You're going to buy the "M" one?

JAKE: Well...uh...not for two grand, but—

NICK: No, it's perfect. You should definitely buy the "M" one. That would be perfect. And we won't tell your wife either. Symmetry.

JAKE: Um. How much...Oh! Look at that. *(Greatly relieved)* "Untitled by "M" is not for sale!" ...Why's that?

NICK: You know, Jake, it's just one of those mysteries.

JAKE: Oh right, the M is for *mystery.* So, you want to go out? Have a drink? The four of us?

NICK: Uh...I think the artists have to stay.

JAKE: But you could go.

NICK: The artist husbands have to stay, too.

(Enter JOANIE *and* MAY.*)*

JOANIE: Here's your magnificent wife back. Thank you for the loan of her. Come on, Nick. Ted's here. He wants to say hello.

NICK: The work of the artist husband is never done. Take care, kids.

*(*NICK *and* JOANIE *exit.)*

JAKE: Damn.

MAY: What?

JAKE: I thought the four of us could go out.

MAY: Which four?

JAKE: You and me and her and Nick.

MAY: Nick? Is that *the* Nick?

JAKE: Yeah. They're married. Figure that. Nick married to a painter.

MAY: *(Astonished)* Oh. Her name is Silver.

JAKE: Maybe she can have two last names to go with her two first names.

MAY: What two first names?

JAKE: *(Points to the paintings.)* "M" and "J". Let's go.

MAY: Uh. We don't have to go. We could stay.

JAKE: I thought you wanted to go.

MAY: I want to look at the picture.

JAKE: *(Mocking)* The "M" one or the "J" one?

MAY: The "M" one.

JAKE: God, why?

MAY: I like to look at it under this nice light.

JAKE: They can't hear you—you don't have to pretend.

MAY: I like it.

JAKE: You don't like it. What's to like about it?

MAY: I like how she looks so sad.

JAKE: I don't see a she.

MAY: That's a lady's face. She looks sad to me.

JAKE: You're losing your mind.

MAY: *(She wants him to see the face.)* Stand further back.

JAKE: I can see it fine.

MAY: You're too close to see the face.

JAKE: You're telling me how to look at a picture—?

MAY: No. I just like looking at it— *(She gets an idea.)*

JAKE: — because I think I can figure out how to look at a picture.

MAY: No, I know. It just...it makes me feel nice.

JAKE: Nice how?

MAY: It kinda turns me on.

JAKE: Jeez—quiet.

MAY: *(Whisper)* No, really. It makes me want to...do it.

JAKE: *(Whisper)* Get out—

MAY: *(Whisper)* No, for real. Maybe it's the angle.

JAKE: Let me stand there.

MAY: Okay, but I want the spot again.

JAKE: Will you get out of the way and let me look at the picture?

(Brief pause. MAY awaits anxiously.)

MAY: ...Do you see it?

JAKE: Will you let me look at this? ...Oh.

MAY: What?

JAKE: It's like a profile. And an apartment building. It's a lady's profile and it's an apartment. And it's sad.

MAY: *(Very happy)* You see that? Do you really see that?

JAKE: Yeah, I see it—calm down, May.

MAY: That's what I see, too.

JAKE: *(Whisper)* But it doesn't make me wanna do it.

MAY: Oh. Just me, I guess. Wanna meet in the bathroom?

8

(*Later.* NICK *awaits* JOANIE *in their living room.*)

(JOANIE *enters.*)

NICK: Why so late? Art patrons overstay their welcome?

JOANIE: I didn't want to leave while Ted was there. People were crowding all over him—I didn't want him to suffocate.

NICK: He knows what he was there to see.

JOANIE: What does that mean?

NICK: ...It means you were the best artist in the show.

JOANIE: He looked at a few of the other paintings. May's.

NICK: Oh yeah—what was that all about?

JOANIE: I had to tell the curators her painting was mine or they never would have hung it. This wasn't a show for students, it was for established artists. Thank goodness her name wasn't on the painting— that guy with her is the bad husband.

NICK: I know him. He's a mechanic. He's been asking around about me. Wanted the four of us to go out for a drink. Jeez.

JOANIE: Is he a thug?

NICK: Well, let's see. I didn't particularly notice thugishness. How would we know that, Joanie?

JOANIE: Some guys are thugs, would you quit being so sensitive?

NICK: Is it like age hair color and weight? "Twenty-five years old, medium build, moderate thugishness?"

JOANIE: A wife is too scared to bring her art home; a wife is not sure she will be able to make every single class; a wife pretends she didn't paint a painting at an art show...those are not good signs. Those are the signs of somebody who gets hit.

NICK: Yeah, okay. Maybe he's a thug. I'll see what I can do. So...any good news?

JOANIE: *Landscape* sold.

NICK: Hey. Congratulations.

JOANIE: Who did you bribe to buy it?

NICK: ...I didn't even know anybody. I swear.

JOANIE: Really?

NICK: Honest to God. *(She beams a repressed beam.)* It was a great turnout. A lot of people got to see your painting.

JOANIE: *(Giddy)* It was completely weird. Who were all those people?

NICK: Just your everyday local art fans. Take that, you fancy downtown gallery owner.

JOANIE: I was sure it was you.

NICK: You always underestimate yourself. It's a great picture.

JOANIE: Thanks. But now I don't have anything for Ted.

NICK: ...What do you mean?

JOANIE: He can't show a painting that's already sold. He said.

NICK: Oh. Oh, yeah. So. What else? Did he say anything else?

JOANIE: He had the custodian refocus the light on my wall. He looked at my wall for a long time.

NICK: At your picture on your wall.

JOANIE: Yes, at my picture on my wall, what else would he be looking at? At May's little student work? He was looking at my work.

NICK: Did he say anything?

JOANIE: "Congratulations, Ms Silver, you have sold a redoubtable piece."

NICK: There, you see?

JOANIE: What's it mean, redoubtable?

NICK: It means really good.

JOANIE: I would rather it was in his gallery.

NICK: No—

JOANIE: Yes. That's why I priced it so high...who's going to pay that for a painting at a high school.

NICK: ...But you feel bad when they don't sell.

JOANIE: I know, but now I don't have anything he wants.

NICK: ...Maybe I could buy it back for you.

JOANIE: Two thousand dollars, Nick.

NICK: Yeah, but it's important to you. Nothing's too good for my baby.

JOANIE: That's okay. *(Bravura)* I'll paint something else. Something new. In the new Joan Silver style.

NICK: ...You weren't too mad I showed up?

JOANIE: What do you mean? I don't get mad when you show up.

NICK: You get mad, *Ms Silver*.

JOANIE: Nick—

NICK: I understand, it's okay.

JOANIE: It's not what you think.

NICK: It isn't?

JOANIE: If you were a lawyer I wouldn't want that known, either.

NICK: Yeah, deep shame there.

JOANIE: Artists live on rice in hovels. Every dime goes to supplies and studio rental, then there's me and Arnold Summerfield's wife...we get a free ride. People don't have to know I don't make a living from my painting. That's the only reason I hide you.

9

(The Lotus Bottom. The next evening)

(JAKE. NICK enters.)

JAKE: Hey, Nick? Right?

NICK: What?!...Oh. You.

JAKE: Jake, yeah. From the garage. And the art show.

NICK: I remember. What are you doing here?

JAKE: Oh, I love The Lotus Bottom. You want a beer? I got two.

NICK: You waiting for somebody?

JAKE: No.

NICK: Why'd you get two?

JAKE: ...So I didn't have to bother him again.

NICK: If I take it, you'll have to bother him again.

JAKE: He doesn't mind. ...Here.

NICK: Thanks.

JAKE: *(Bravura)* Oh, no, it's on me.

NICK: *(Who hasn't reached for his wallet)* Yeah, I know. So. Jake, right?

JAKE: Jake. That's me. Jake.

NICK: I've never seen you in here before, Jake.

JAKE: Yeah, I come here. Yeah, I like it.

NICK: It's a dump.

JAKE: Except for that part. May likes it.

NICK: May...The girl who is not an art student?

JAKE: She's my wife.

NICK: Uh huh.

(An awkward pause for JAKE*)*

JAKE: We're going to get re-married in the church.

NICK: Oh yeah, otherwise you'll never hear the end of it. Me and Joanie were going to elope. You'd have thought we'd announced terrorist plans. Her parents, boy.

JAKE: This is for me.

NICK: Oh.

JAKE: I want to join up.

NICK: ...I'm sorry...you want to what?

JAKE: Join the church.

NICK: Oh. I thought you wanted to join the *army* and wanted to get married in the church before you left for parts unknown. I'm sorry, my brain. What? You're going to convert?

JAKE: I think so.

NICK: For your wife.

JAKE: Yeah. I want to fit in.

NICK: With her family.

JAKE: They're dead.

NICK: Uh huh.

JAKE: *(Pointedly)* With the neighborhood.

NICK: Ah.

JAKE: Yeah. So I fit in. With you know...

NICK: Oh, yes, I see. You want to fit in with the neighborhood. With certain elements of the neighborhood. I see, yes. Okay...

(NICK realizes JAKE wants a job. Decides to take advantage of the situation.)

NICK: Joining the church is not necessarily the best way to fit in.

JAKE: You go, don't you? To church?

NICK: I come here, too, but I don't recommend it. There are other ways you could maybe fit in...what's your wife think about it?

JAKE: I don't know.

NICK: Shouldn't you ask her? What wives think is very important.

JAKE: Oh, I know. I know that.

NICK: What does she do, your wife?

JAKE: She's a wife.

NICK: All day?

JAKE: She has her hair done. She goes to Curves.

NICK: You got kids?

JAKE: We're not ready.

NICK: The church might not like that.

JAKE: Oh, yeah, I heard. You have kids?

NICK: We're not ready. But Joanie is an artist.

JAKE: They don't have kids?

NICK: Well, they do, but if they don't they're still occupied. Art takes all day.

JAKE: Oh, yeah, I can see that.

NICK: And all night sometimes, too. Like that show. That show took a lot of Joanie's time.

JAKE: Sure.

NICK: I'm going to be frank with you, Jake.

JAKE: Yes, please.

NICK: There are some selfish benefits to having your wife be an artist.

JAKE: What are they?

NICK: I've noticed that when she is working on a painting she never criticizes, never notices that my pants don't match, I didn't shave, my fingernails are dirty. Soon as the painting's done, here it comes.

JAKE: May doesn't criticize.

NICK: But she thinks it. Little silent opinions.

JAKE: Silent?

NICK: And little. They all think them. Your clothes, your weight—well not you, the weight—your eating habits—

JAKE: Table manners?

NICK: Fiber intake.

JAKE: You think she thinks that?

NICK: She wouldn't if she were an artist.

JAKE: Yeah, but she's not.

NICK: Too bad, Jake. It makes you look good, when your wife is an artist.

JAKE: How?

NICK: Well. For one thing, it reveals a great deal of culture, to have a wife with paintings. It puts you into a whole new social world. Contacts. Networking with other...C E Os.

JAKE: Uh huh.

NICK: Uh huh. Art...takes up a whole lot of space.

JAKE: In the apartment.

NICK: No. In her brain and in her heart. So that she gets to feel fulfilled. Art fills up her day and fills up her heart. So that she is happy.

JAKE: Oh, yeah.

NICK: Making sure your wife is happy is part of being a man.

JAKE: Hey, I make her plenty happy. She's happy.

NICK: ...I don't mean *that*.

JAKE: What? ...What do you mean?

NICK: Part of being a man...a real man...means you're happy when your wife takes art lessons.

JAKE: I guess I never thought of that.

NICK: It's one of the checks, how a guy can check if he's a good husband. A check list, you know what I mean?

JAKE: Uh...no.

NICK: A list to check off. A check off list. Am-I-doing-a-good-job-as-a-husband list to check off... Do I share all my money with my wife? Check. How about you, can you check that one?

JAKE: Uh, sure, check.

NICK: *(Pointedly)* I never hit my wife. Check.

JAKE: Uh huh.

NICK: It's a check list, Jake. Not an uh-huh list.

JAKE: I'd never hit May.

NICK: I never hit my wife, check.

JAKE: Check.

NICK: ...Check. I'm happy when my wife takes art lessons. Check. *(Brief pause.)* Check?

JAKE: I can't check it—she doesn't take them!

NICK: Joanie gives lessons, you know.

JAKE: What kind of lessons?

NICK: Art lessons, man—! What are we talking about here! Get your wife some art lessons.

10

(Later. JAKE in bed. MAY is off.)

JAKE: I was thinking about it, uh today...and I thought that you should. Maybe you should take some art—

(MAY enters in sexy sleepwear. JAKE is impressed.)

JAKE: What's that?

MAY: Baby dolls.

JAKE: They're good.

MAY: Forty dollars.

JAKE: Don't tell me how much they cost.

MAY: I thought you should know—

JAKE: It spoils the mood.

MAY: It's your money.

JAKE: No, it isn't.

MAY: It isn't your money?

JAKE: No, it is not. It's our money.

MAY: Since when?

JAKE: What do you mean?

MAY: I mean, "I'm the one with the job, May".

JAKE: I never said that.

MAY: Jake!

JAKE: Well, I'm sorry if I said it. It's your money, too. You have the right...to do what you want...with your money.

MAY: I didn't earn it.

JAKE: You're my wife. So it's all community property.

MAY: ...Are we getting a divorce?

JAKE: We're not getting a divorce.

MAY: Okay, good, I didn't know, "community property," I thought we were getting some divorce I don't know about.

JAKE: No. We're moving into a new stage.

MAY: A stage where we share your money?

JAKE: Our money. Everything that comes into this house is fifty-fifty. From now on.

MAY: Who have you been talking to?

JAKE: Nobody.

MAY: Is this supposed to mean more blow jobs?

JAKE: I don't like to hear you say that, it is not attractive to me at all.

MAY: I'm trying it out.

JAKE: Trying what out?

MAY: Saying it. Blow job.

JAKE: May.

MAY: B J.

JAKE: What's got into you?

MAY: Blow job. Try it.

JAKE: Try what?

MAY: Say it.

JAKE: I can't say that.

MAY: You've never said blow job in your life?

JAKE: Never.

MAY: At the garage, you never say May gives me blow jobs?

JAKE: We're married.

MAY: There were some unmarried blow jobs.

JAKE: I am not listening to this.

MAY: Were they better? The unmarried blow jobs?

JAKE: Jesus, May.

MAY: The priest hates it when you say Jesus.

JAKE: He likes it when you say...that other word?

MAY: Blow job?

JAKE: Yeah.

MAY: It's two words.

JAKE: *(Brief pause)* They were not better.

MAY: What wasn't better?

JAKE: The unmarried ones.

MAY: I have no idea what you're talking about.

JAKE: May!

MAY: Really, what are you talking about, Jake? What wasn't better?

JAKE: I'm not going to do this.

MAY: Do what?

JAKE: I'm not going to say it.

MAY: Okay. Then I'm not going under the covers.

JAKE: ...You'll go under the covers if I say it?

MAY: Could be.

JAKE: Can I talk first?

MAY: You can talk during.

JAKE: ...Blow job.

MAY: I'm sorry, what did you say?

JAKE: Blow job.

MAY: Hm?

JAKE: Blow job blow job blow job.

(MAY *goes under the covers.*)

JAKE: You know...May...I think you should take some art...some art classes.

(JAKE, *too, goes under the covers, as they both start to giggle.*)

11

(*The next day.* NICK *and* JOANIE *at Ted's downtown art gallery.*)

(*They are dressed up and slightly in disguise, hats and sunglasses.* JOANIE *looks at paintings.* NICK *approaches.*)

NICK: You can take them off. He's not here.

JOANIE: I don't want him to recognize me.

NICK: Joanie, Ted is not here. He's on vacation. Take off your sunglasses. You're making people nervous.

JOANIE: What? They think we're art thieves?

NICK: Sunglasses inside make people nervous.

JOANIE: Do I look like an art thief to you?

NICK: I don't know what an art thief looks like. I just feel very silly.

JOANIE: You can be in an art gallery, Nick. You don't have to feel silly.

NICK: I know I can be in an art gallery, Joanie—I don't want to be sneaking around in an art gallery. I don't like how it looks.

JOANIE: We do not look like art thieves. Art thieves wear masks. What self respecting art thief would steal any of these paintings? Would you steal that painting?

NICK: I wouldn't steal any painting.

JOANIE: Would you steal that one?

NICK: No, Joanie, I wouldn't.

JOANIE: I wouldn't steal any of these paintings.

NICK: ...What about that one?

JOANIE: ...I wouldn't steal it.

NICK: No, I wouldn't steal it, but...it's interesting. We could buy it. Do you want to buy it?

JOANIE: Buy it, Nick? We don't buy paintings. *(Pause as she looks at it.)* I couldn't live with it. *(Brief pause)* You couldn't live with it.

NICK: Why not?

JOANIE: It's too...it's too something. *(Pleading)* You couldn't live with it, Nick, you couldn't.

NICK: ...You're right. I couldn't live with it. What was I thinking—but somebody can live with it. *(Points)* Red dot.

JOANIE: Somebody's going to put that in their house? What room? Not the bedroom, my god, you couldn't sleep; not the living room, you couldn't...live. The dungeon room? I can't believe somebody bought it. *(Brief pause)* Nobody bought it. It wouldn't still be here if somebody bought it.

NICK: *(Placating)* You're right. Maybe it's not for sale. They put the red dot on it so nobody would try to buy it.

JOANIE: Who? All the people with dungeons—? Why would anybody buy this? There isn't any light in it.

NICK: There's no color.

JOANIE: It just sort of sucks you in like a black hole. Is this what they want now, this soul-sucking black hole?

NICK: You're way better than this. Your stuff.

JOANIE: I paint light.

NICK: You're known for that.

JOANIE: ...How does he do that, that sucking swirling thing? It's the shades he uses, the dark shades.

NICK: It's way too dark.

JOANIE: Not really, not when you think about the light that isn't there. When you think about the light that isn't there, it's not too dark at all... You know, Nick, darkness is just another form of light. Another kind of light. Really...dark is the opposite of light and it couldn't be opposite unless it were actually the same.

NICK: Uh huh. Let's go get some lunch.

JOANIE: It would be fun, wouldn't it, Nick? To drink champagne here, on the first Friday evening of the month, surrounded by Joan Silver paintings.

END OF ACT ONE

ACT TWO

1

(The next day. The studio)

(JOANIE takes photographs of her new painting. MAY enters with a painting of her own.)

JOANIE: How did you get in the building?

MAY: The door's open.

JOANIE: Most people buzz.

MAY: Most people walk in and steal. Why are you taking pictures?

JOANIE: ...So I can send the transparencies to an art dealer.

MAY: *(Impressed.)* Oh, man. Can I look?

JOANIE: Sure.

(MAY looks at JOANIE's painting.)

MAY: What is that? That is not what you show us in class.

JOANIE: ...It's too advanced for class...

MAY: Kind of dark. ...Really dark.

JOANIE: Yes, the darkness pulls you in. The swirls pull you down. Do you feel it? Do you feel sucked down?

MAY: I don't know. I don't think I feel sucked down.

JOANIE: ...Did you forget something, May? Did you leave something here? I didn't find anything.

MAY: I want to paint.

JOANIE: There's no class today.

MAY: I won't take up any room at all. Just my table.

JOANIE: I can't have you looking over my shoulder.

MAY: Hey, I'm not going to copy your idea. I don't even get it. I'll be way over there. I'll be really quiet.

JOANIE: You're the noisiest student I have.

MAY: Yeah. The paint sort of takes over—I hear this music in my head—must be why people paint and knit and draw and all—for the music. I just want to keep it going—could I come when you're done? I know you can't paint all day—the hand goes.

JOANIE: Goes where?

MAY: Four or five hours, it starts to cramp.

JOANIE: Four or five hours?

MAY: Yeah. Is that about how long it is for you? I mean you're older and all.

(*Brief pause.* JOANIE *takes* MAY's *canvas.*)

JOANIE: Where did this one come from?

MAY: I started it in class yesterday.

JOANIE: ...What is this?

MAY: It's the face.

JOANIE: Where?

MAY: All over. (*Points*) Nose. Eye. Mouth. Lips. Do you see it?

JOANIE: I see it... (*She is awed by the painting.*)

MAY: I think I started to really get it with this one. The art thing. It felt really good, sexy, almost. And everything just flowed out of me. It felt like in November when it gets a little colder and the light comes through the trees. I did it all at once really fast. I felt...smart. And I felt...artistic.

JOANIE: Oh, May.

MAY: What?

JOANIE: That's the deception. When it feels like that. Painting is one part inspiration and nine parts sweat equity. You have to learn some craft. Learn the craft and apply it to your inspiration. Otherwise you're a mockery. A laughing stock. Put your inspiration on the back burner while I teach you some craft.

MAY: Why?

JOANIE: Because your inspiration will lead you down a garden path and abandon you. I can't let that happen to you. Craft will never abandon you. I don't know how to tell you this—there's no other way to say it—this is just...crap. I think you have some talent, but this, this you must throw this away. It's backsliding.

MAY: You think I have talent?

JOANIE: Yes. Little Miss Slut Shirt has talent. But you have to get technique. You must work on your technique. Are you willing to do that? Will you work on technique?

MAY: Little Miss who?

JOANIE: Nothing, it's just a saying, an art saying— (Laughs) "Flows out of you." Art does not flow out of you. Art...isn't endorphins—I never got *them* either.

MAY: What are they—?

JOANIE: And I jogged for a long time. We'll throw this away.

MAY: No—could I just—

JOANIE: No. You must be bold. Art takes boldness. And technique. You can't just paint what's in your mind. One day you will try to paint what's in your mind and nothing will be there, and without technique you will simply not be able to go forward. You will be stuck there, in your mind. With technique, you can paint what you see in the world. A puddle, a ripple on a lake. Water is hard to paint. Puddles, mud. They reflect the light. You must have technique to paint them. Anything you see in the world takes technique to paint.

MAY: Okay.

JOANIE: No more improvisation. Paint what I teach. No more face. Let the face wait, it isn't going anywhere.

MAY: And I can come here? Like when you're done? I can come and paint?

JOANIE: Of course. Artists take care of their disciples.

MAY: Great. I was turning my apartment into a disaster area.

JOANIE: But—. You said you had to do everything in secret.

MAY: I don't have to now.

JOANIE: Your husband will get pissed off.

MAY: (Surprised) He won't get pissed off.

JOANIE: Yes, he'll hit you.

MAY: He—no! He doesn't hit me. He doesn't get pissed off. I didn't want him to know about the lessons because I didn't want him to feel bad.

JOANIE: About what?

MAY: He doesn't have anything. Neither one of us, nothing, we're nothing. If I all of a sudden got art and Jake didn't have anything, he'd feel left out.

JOANIE: You were protecting his feelings?

MAY: I figured I could take lessons until I got Ma's face, and he'd never have to know. Or maybe by then he'd get some hobby, too.

JOANIE: *(Almost choking)* Hobby?

MAY: *(Really happy)* Yeah. I never had a hobby before. I never knew how fun it could be.

JOANIE: Well, what happened? Did Jake get a *hobby*, too?

MAY: No, it's all changed. I thought you knew.

JOANIE: Knew what?

MAY: Nick. Nick told Jake about how he should let me get art lessons. I didn't tell him I already had.

JOANIE: My Nick talked to your husband about your art classes?

MAY: They had some conversation.

JOANIE: Oh. Well. Sure, they had some conversation.

MAY: Where are you going?

JOANIE: To have a little conversation of my own.

2

(Meanwhile. NICK *in his office)*

*(*JAKE *enters.)*

JAKE: Uh, Hi.

NICK: ...Hi.

JAKE: These were on the floor out there, these quarters. I thought I should turn them in.

NICK: You can put them on the desk.

JAKE: Oh, hey. It looks good there.

NICK: Kind of red for the room, but yeah.

JAKE: Are these other ones hers, too?

NICK: Yes.

JAKE: They look good.... She doesn't know they're here?

NICK: She has no idea. She hangs them in a restaurant owned by a pal of mine. Every few weeks one disappears from the restaurant wall and comes to live on these walls and Joanie receives a check in the mail. It's a nightmare for my tax accountant. What can I do for you, Jake?

JAKE: Oh, I'm sorry. Are you busy?

NICK: I am expecting a call.

JAKE: I'll come back.

NICK: Why don't we wait until the phone rings. In the meantime you can tell me what you have on your mind.

JAKE: I wanted to thank you for the tip. The art lessons. May is really happy.

NICK: That's what we all live for. To make our wives happy.

JAKE: That's what I live for

NICK: Well, you're welcome. Anything else? *(Pause)* What is it, Jake?

JAKE: I'm sort of fed up. With the garage.

NICK: Fixing a car is a beautiful thing. It's a skill that can take you any place on the planet. And it's a good living.

JAKE: It's not the money.

NICK: Having a problem with the boss?

JAKE: The boss loves me.

NICK: Can't get along with your coworkers?

JAKE: It's not like that. They all want to partner with me. I can smell a problem, I don't have to hook the car up to the computer. I listen, I sniff, I fix. Everybody wants to learn that. I don't know how to teach it, though.

NICK: That's because you can't teach a gift. You have a gift. I promise you, you leave the garage you'll miss it every day.

JAKE: I got to think of my future. Someday I'll be thirty. Some day I'll be *forty*. I don't want to be climbing under cars when I'm old.

NICK: *(Amused)* Start saving your money. Stick with the cars. You'll retire at fifty.

JAKE: ...It's for May.

NICK: ...May... Having a little opinion is she? About all the grease you bring home?

JAKE: No. I mean, I don't think she is. It's so I can be a better husband for May. *(Brief pause)* You know, "Check?"

NICK: For May, huh? ...Okay. Do you have any experience in banking?

JAKE: Banking? It's a bank back there?

NICK: It's gambling.

JAKE: Then why do I need banking experience?

NICK: The guys working the phones, they're mostly former tellers.

JAKE: I don't have banking. But I'm pretty strong.

NICK: It's not like the old days. We don't use muscle. We use technology. Our clients have accounts. They win, we credit the account. They lose, we debit the account. The account is at zero, we do not take the wager. It's all good now. No problems with clients not paying, no problem with tellers cheating. It's all clean and nice. Every day, we check the books. They always add up. It's beautiful. But you need banking experience to work for me.

JAKE: I'm a very fast learner. I hope you will give me a chance. I even prayed for it. Outside the church.

(The phone rings. They listen.)

NICK: I got to get this.

(It rings.)

NICK: Okay, Jake. Come back Friday.

JAKE: Thank you, Mister D, thanks a lot.

(JAKE exits. The phone rings again, NICK picks it up.)

NICK: Talk to me—and do not tell me I still have a tenant.... Good. What did the guys have to do? Really? Is the dryer okay? (Laughs) Good. Very good.

(JOANIE enters. NICK is on the phone and doesn't see her yet. She, in amazement, looks at the art on the walls.)

NICK: I also want the unit upstairs. Find out who's up there and what it's gonna take to get them out. *(Laughs)* Yeah, that's one of the perks of being in the laundry business. *(Sees* JOANIE*)* ...I gotta go.

*(*JOANIE *turns slowly as she looks at all of her paintings.)*

NICK: Joanie—listen to me.

JOANIE: I am such a fool.

NICK: I love you.

JOANIE: *(Looking at a painting)* I always imagined this in some small entry way; the penthouse. You get off the private elevator and this is staring at you. You look at it while you're waiting for your elegant hostess to open the door.

NICK: Joanie—

JOANIE: I'm really glad to see it again. Funny, though. It's better in my mind than it really is. Maybe I should go deeper into my mind while I'm trying to paint them. But then, there's always the chance that if I go too deep I'll find the void, the place where there's nothing there any more. Just vapid empty Joanie da Silva.

NICK: You're not empty.

JOANIE: Where are the rest of them? ...What? You threw them away? Only kept the ones that don't threaten you?

NICK: They all threaten me. Every single one of them.

JOANIE: Where are the rest?

NICK: Back there.

JOANIE: What's back there?

NICK: The phones.

JOANIE: Oh. Sure. The boys on the phones need culture, too. Or maybe they function as dart boards.

NICK: You're so unhappy when they don't sell.

JOANIE: I really am an idiot. Who buys a two thousand dollar painting off the wall of a high school?

NICK: Somebody who loves it.

JOANIE: You don't love it. You don't even understand it.

NICK: I love you.

JOANIE: Stay away from me. Stay out of my life. Leave my students alone.

NICK: I don't—

JOANIE: Oh please, Nick. You expect me to believe anything you say?

NICK: I bought the paintings. I didn't do anything else.

JOANIE: You talked to Jake—don't deny it, I just saw him leave.

NICK: I was trying to help! I was doing what you want—I'm keeping an eye on him—making sure he doesn't hit his wife. So what, I talked to *Jake*. I never talked to that idiot *Ted*—I could have taken Ted around the bend, the way he talked to you, like you're a kid. You think it was easy for me to watch him sneer at your pictures. I couldn't have him thinking nobody buys your pictures.

JOANIE: He sneered? ...What do you mean he sneered? ...Oh, my God. What did he say?

NICK: Nothing. He didn't say anything. I didn't like the way he looked, that's all.

JOANIE: ...I am a total laughing stock.

NICK: You're not a laughing stock.

JOANIE: What? You think he doesn't know who bought it? You think that's some secret you have?

NICK: Ted doesn't know. None of those other panties know. I am very careful. I think you should appreciate what I do for you.

JOANIE: Panties?

NICK: You don't like them either. Those stuffed shirts, bringing their important opinions to the masses— like we're a bunch of peasants—who needs them?

JOANIE: You...You are out of my life. Out of my life.

3

(The next evening. MAY *and* JAKE's *bedroom.*

*(*MAY's *giving* JAKE *a manicure.)*

MAY: It didn't matter at the garage, but maybe it matters for phone work.

JAKE: A bunch of guys are not going to care about my fingernails.

MAY: You'd be surprised what people care about.

JAKE: It's very busy there, May. No time to be looking at somebody else's hands.

MAY: They'll look during smoke breaks.

JAKE: No smoking allowed.

MAY: You're kidding.

JAKE: It's very classy.

MAY: Oh, sure.

JAKE: They wear ties.

MAY: That's exactly my point. Men in ties don't have car grease under their nails. You don't want to give them a reason to look down on you.

JAKE: It's a room full of bookies. Who's going to look down?

MAY: ...Jake, the new guy from out of town, walks in, doesn't know the ropes, has grease under his nails? I'm just sayin'.

JAKE: ...Yeah, okay. Get the thumb.

MAY: I will.

JAKE: *(Brief pause.)* Did you...did you ever think anything?

MAY: About what?

JAKE: About all the grease.

MAY: What do you mean?

JAKE: Did you, like, have some...opinion about that?

MAY: I don't remember an opinion.

JAKE: Some silent little opinion?

MAY: I don't have those.

JAKE: But you noticed.

MAY: Sure, I always noticed.

JAKE: You noticed, but you didn't think anything?

MAY: I don't think so.

JAKE: You didn't think, wow that is one nasty hand. I hope he doesn't put it inside me. It will be gross if he touches me with that grease-creased hand. Boy, I wish he'd get the grease off before he gets into bed tonight.

MAY: Jake—

JAKE: Or maybe close your eyes so you don't have to look?

MAY: I don't close my eyes, you know that. ...Maybe I had an opinion. But maybe it wasn't a bad one. "Oh, please let him put that greasy hand inside me."

JAKE: I don't like that kind of talk.

MAY: You started it.

JAKE: I did not.

MAY: You said grease on the hand that goes inside me. *(Playing)* Greasy hand, greasy hand, how I love your greasy hand.

JAKE: You're kidding, right?

MAY: *(Breathy)* Greasy hands, greasy hands.

JAKE: May!

MAY: Of course, I'm kidding.

JAKE: Oh. Okay.

MAY: A little.

JAKE: May!

MAY: I love you, I don't care about grease. Jeez. Here, I got you some shirts. They take ties.

JAKE: I'm going to wear the knits.

MAY: You can see your nipples.

JAKE: I don't have nipples.

MAY: You look like a hood in the knits.

JAKE: It's not even my birthday.

MAY: Do you like them?

JAKE: Yeah. So you're glad? About the job?

MAY: I am not glad.

JAKE: You bought me shirts.

MAY: Not from gladness.

JAKE: What from?

MAY: From you need them. From I don't want you to be embarrassed. From I'm your wife I think about you.

JAKE: *(Brief pause)* Do you think about me when you paint?

MAY: No.

JAKE: What do you think about?

MAY: I don't want to talk about it. You said it was alright—I should take lessons—so I take them—I don't want to talk about it—you said it was alright—

JAKE: It's fine, it's fine, jeez. I just want to know what you think about. What were you thinking when you painted the purple one with the tunnels?

MAY: What tunnels?

JAKE: The tunnels. The two train tunnels leading into very deep darkness. What was going through your mind?

(A kind of joyous glee in JAKE *and* MAY *increases from here.)*

MAY: They're nostrils. They're not train tunnels. You thought they were train tunnels?

JAKE: Nostrils. And that thing between them is nose? What were you thinking?

MAY: I don't know—What do you think about when you ream an engine?!

JAKE: You.

MAY: You do not.

JAKE: I do, too. The car is...uh...

MAY: The car is what?

JAKE: The car is *coming*...and oozing all over me.

MAY: Jake!

JAKE: It makes me think of your ooze. That's why I don't wash.

MAY: You are lying—you are so lying.

JAKE: Why do you say that?

MAY: Because I've been there, I have been right there. "Boy that fucking car busted my balls. Boy that caddy was a piece of shit. Boy, why would anybody in his right mind buy a car from Korea." You were not thinking about me coming all over your hands when you got covered in car juice. What are you smiling about?

JAKE: I didn't know you paid that much attention.

MAY: I'm your wife!

JAKE: Doesn't mean you pay attention. Are they my nostrils?

MAY: No.

JAKE: Do you paint me?

MAY: *(Closer and closer toward a kiss)* I do not paint you. I do not paint you. I do not paint you, Jake.

5

(A few days later. NICK's *office)*

*(*JAKE *is remorseful.)*

NICK: Why was it so big? It was so big because Barry the Weasel had some inside tip.

JAKE: The race was fixed?

NICK: Fixed or not fixed that is not our problem. Our problem, yours and mine, is how did you come up with the amount of money we paid Barry McClanahan? Did you use the calculator?

JAKE: I thought I did.

NICK: The number seven went off at eight to one.
So Barry's winnings are ten thousand times eight which
is eighty thousand dollars, less our eighteen percent.

JAKE: Um—

NICK: Oh. You added.

JAKE: I did?

NICK: Yes. You added our vig to Barry's winnings,
thus giving Barry ninety-four thousand four hundred
dollars instead of sixty-five thousand six hundred
dollars. You overpaid in the amount of twenty-eight
thousand eight hundred dollars.

(Pause)

JAKE: You *subtract* the vig?

NICK: You subtract it from the winnings! And we keep
it, it is our cut. If he loses, we get his whole wager.
But he won, so we only get our vig. We always get
something. When you add instead of subtract you cheat
us out of almost thirty thousand dollars. We must never
be cheated out of almost thirty thousand dollars.

JAKE: I explained to him how it was a math error.

NICK: Yes you did. But the weasel has already
withdrawn the money from his account and has
no intention of paying us back.

JAKE: Oh.

NICK: The upside is that the weasel will probably want
to wager on football before the weekend, and we will
not take his bet until this bank error in his favor is
addressed. We will get back our twenty-eight thousand
eight hundred dollars. So. You have it now, don't you?
You understand the math now, don't you?

JAKE: I do.

NICK: Okay. No more math mistakes.

JAKE: ...Are the guys all laughing at me or what?

NICK: Nobody laughs at mistakes. Everybody takes mistakes very seriously. Everything stops. We check everything. Nobody is laughing.

JAKE: But they blame me.

NICK: They are so relieved that it was your mistake and not their mistake that they are grateful. They are grateful to you, Jake. Do not worry about what the guys are thinking. That is the least of your worries.

JAKE: No, it's not me. I'm not worried. It's May. She worries that somebody might look down.

NICK: May. May is worried about you at your work? Having a little silent opinion, is she?

JAKE: Oh, no. She doesn't have those.

NICK: Uh huh. Not having any problems at home, are you?

JAKE: No no.

NICK: You weren't, for example, thinking about home problems when you made this math error? Some little silent opinion about some minuscule Jake mistake because your shirt is too orange, it is too orange and this little orange mistake erupts into a mountain? A mountain of wifely opinion?

JAKE: No, it's not like that, it wasn't May.

NICK: What wasn't May? What is it, Jake? Spit it out.

JAKE: I might have been thinking of something. Something not math.

NICK: Yeees?

JAKE: An electrical circuit—the electrical circuit in the '85 Mustang I was fixing when I quit the garage. I realized it was a cracked battery casing, which explains why it wouldn't hold the charge—not the belt. That's what I was thinking. Not May.

NICK: But you won't think that any more, will you?

JAKE: No.

NICK: No. It would be a very terrible mistake to be thinking about a Mustang battery while you are trying to figure out Barry McClanahan's vigorish. Imagine if you make a second math mistake? How that mistake might be corrected.

JAKE: I'd pay it out of my salary?

NICK: Oh. ...At the very least.

5

(Later. The art studio)

(JOANIE is working. NICK enters.)

NICK: Hi.

JOANIE: Couldn't you buzz?

NICK: I didn't want you to have to stop working.

JOANIE: But it didn't work did it?, because, look, I have stopped. Next time ring the bell.

NICK: I brought your mail—there's a letter from the gallery.

(JOANIE takes, opens and reads the letter, slides tumble out. NICK picks them up, holds them to the light.)

NICK: These look very professional... What's he say?

JOANIE: It doesn't concern you. Give me those. *(She takes the slides, rips them up with the letter.)*

NICK: Okay. *(He looks at the new paintings.)* These are good.

JOANIE: *(Sarcasm)* Oh yeah, just ask Ted how good they are.

NICK: *(Adamant)* They are good. They are different, and they are good.

JOANIE: *(Brief pause, hopeful)* ...Not so literal.

NICK: Yes. Not literal. Emotional. I like them. A lot. *(Brief pause)* Where do you sleep?

JOANIE: The sofa opens.

NICK: It opens?

JOANIE: It opens.

NICK: Did we ever open it?

JOANIE: No. We were going to once, but we made them stay in a hotel.

NICK: Who were they?

JOANIE: Some cousins from Wisconsin.

NICK: You have cousins in Wisconsin?

JOANIE: Your cousin Lester! With the garage in Kenosha!

NICK: Oh, yeah, Lester and Bride Number Four. Thank god he put the garage in my name before she took him to the cleaners.

JOANIE: ...Do you have any opinions about any other marriages I should know about?

NICK: ...No, I have no opinions whatsoever— So it's comfortable, the sofa-bed?

JOANIE: It's a sofa-bed, Nick.

NICK: I'll send a couple guys over with the bed.

JOANIE: I don't want your guys coming here.

NICK: I can't carry it myself.

JOANIE: If I want a bed I'll go to Sleepworld.

NICK: So. You don't want the bed. Did you just...
I don't know...want to see me?

JOANIE: Here.

(JOANIE *hands* NICK *a check.*)

NICK: What's this for?

JOANIE: I think your guys have laughed enough at
my expense.

NICK: Nobody laughs at you.

JOANIE: I want them back.

NICK: You're buying your pictures off me?

JOANIE: Yes.

NICK: This isn't enough.

JOANIE: It's what you paid.

NICK: They're more valuable now.

JOANIE: Because I'm such a famous artist?

NICK: You're more famous, and how much I love them.
They are worth a great deal more to me than this.

JOANIE: I want them.

NICK: *(Tears up check)* ...You may borrow them back.
Anything else?

JOANIE: I'm filing for divorce.

NICK: No.

JOANIE: You can't stop me.

(NICK *laughs quietly.*)

JOANIE: Don't do this.

NICK: Da Silvas don't get divorces. My mother tried to divorce my father.

JOANIE: She did not.

NICK: Early on. She kept leaving to live with relatives who would then die off.

JOANIE: Did your father kill them?

NICK: No, they were old. Well, one or two he might have killed—I'm kidding. She finally gave up. After a certain age, there's no point in divorce. What, you think you're going to change, go be different with some other guy? You're not going to change. It'll be the same thing all over again. You'll fall in love with some guy who's just like me. Might as well stay with me.

JOANIE: This isn't about some guy, some other guy. I don't want a guy, are you kidding?

NICK: What's it about then?

JOANIE: What do you think it's about?!

NICK: ...What? Guilty, your honor. I bought her paintings and hung them in my office—

JOANIE: You lied to me.

NICK: That's no reason for a divorce.

JOANIE: *(Blurting)* "I don't like what he does for a living, your honor." How's that for a reason.

NICK: *(Pause, feigned sympathy)* Oh, sweetheart, sweetie. No.

JOANIE: Don't make me get ugly, Nick.

(NICK laughs.)

JOANIE: Damn it. Damn you. Damn it.

6

(The next day. An outdoor art show at the zoo. JOANIE *with her paintings on display.)*

*(*MAY *enters.)*

MAY: Mrs Silver— Hi, oh my God, Hi! You're not going to believe this—I never knew they allowed paintings at the zoo.

JOANIE: What are you doing? Why are you here?

MAY: We walked by the church, and all these artists had their stuff out, it was amazing, I never saw art on the street. Some girl said, "What? You've never been to the zoo?" And I never had. She said anybody can set up a table. Well, I don't have a table so I brought a picture and a guy let me show it at his table. I sold it. I sold my picture for a hundred dollars. I was going to ask for ten, but the table guy, he did all the talking.

JOANIE: You sold a painting?

MAY: Yeah. But, now I wish I had it back. Isn't that weird. I didn't think about it, I just sold it. I'm not going to do it again. I don't know how you can part with them. Isn't this great? It's like a great big Farmers' Market but it's art instead of vegetables! Are these all yours?

JOANIE: Of course they're all mine.

MAY: They're all so different.

JOANIE: There are several periods represented. Several different periods of exploration in my work.

MAY: I didn't know you sold your pictures here. Cool.

JOANIE: No, I don't sell my paintings here, not usually. I show them in a very exclusive restaurant.

MAY: Where is it? Me and Jake—

JOANIE: No, no, they're not there any more, they're here. I brought them here, but they're really much too expensive for the street.

MAY: What is?

JOANIE: My paintings—

MAY: Oh—how much...my God. People pay that? On the street?

JOANIE: ...That's what they're worth. We have to charge what they're worth.

MAY: Wow. How many have you sold?

JOANIE: Just a few. A very few. I didn't bring them to sell. I bring them—I brought them today, because I don't usually bring them, they usually hang in the restaurant, I brought them because I've gotten too estranged, too estranged from the struggle. I thought it would be good to remind myself. Of the struggle.

MAY: What struggle?

JOANIE: The struggle artists go through to sell their work!

MAY: Oh.

JOANIE: The competition. The marketplace.

MAY: Yeah. Look at all these artists.

JOANIE: Not just these ones. Galleries, the internet, the street, the world...it's very competitive.

MAY: Yeah. Must be horrible. Still, it's a nice day to be outside.

JOANIE: I could lower the prices—

MAY: Sure. I got a hundred dollars.

JOANIE: But we mustn't do that. We can't be giving it away. We must sell it for what it's worth. I get thousands for these. In the restaurant.

MAY: But if you don't sell them you have to carry them all home again.

JOANIE: That's why there are taxis.

MAY: At the Farmers' Market they lower the prices at the end of the day. So they don't have to pack up all the vegetables and take them home. You could try that.

7

(Meanwhile. NICK's office)

(NICK is taking the paintings down. JAKE enters.)

JAKE: I subtracted. I checked every payout. I didn't make any errors—

NICK: Great. Hold this.

(NICK hands JAKE a painting and climbs down.)

JAKE: Did I make another mistake?

NICK: God, I hope not.

JAKE: Oh. I thought that's why you called me in. *(Brief pause)* We moving?

NICK: The paintings are moving. Temporarily.

JAKE: ...I'll miss them.

NICK: So will I. You know how to drive the Titan?

JAKE: Oh sure. We drove it at the garage. ...I mean. We had to road test it.

NICK: Yes, you had to road test it two hundred and sixty miles.

JAKE: That wasn't me.

NICK: Drive these over to the studio. The rest are in the truck.

JAKE: Okay. ...I thought she didn't know you had them—

NICK: Don't think.

JAKE: Okay. Is that one you?

NICK: *(Amazement)* What?

JAKE: That face. Is it you?

NICK: I have no idea.

JAKE: I always thought it was you.

NICK: You did? I never even... *(Looking hard at it)* She never said it was me.

JAKE: I was a little jealous. Your wife paints you. My wife doesn't paint me.

NICK: It's cubist.

JAKE: Who's he?

NICK: *(Lost in the painting)* Maybe it is me. Maybe that's why she wants it back...subconsciously.... A picture to remind her of me.

JAKE: It reminds me of you—

NICK: Why would she need to paint me when she has me? Isn't the real thing good enough, she's got to reinvent it in squares? I'll keep this one. There's so many. Maybe she won't notice.

JAKE: I won't say anything.

NICK: All those times she's off in her own world, maybe I'm there too. Little bits of me sneaking into the corners. That's why there's no frames, she doesn't want to cover me up.

JAKE: *(Uncomfortable)* I'm going to go now.

NICK: Don't let her see you sweat. If your knees start to collapse, just lock 'em.

JAKE: They won't do that—

NICK: When your stomach sinks, make your face a rock, your jaw a smirk, act like you own all the rules. Because if she knows, if she knows how you are dying inside, she'll have all the cards.

JAKE: Okay, Nick...I'm going, okay?

NICK: *(Crestfallen.)* She is not leaving me. She is not.

8

(The next day. The studio)

(JOANIE paints. MAY enters with another new painting.)

MAY: Was that the gallery guy?

JOANIE: *(Caught)* Was who the gallery guy?

MAY: The guy I met at the art show. The gallery guy. He was getting into a taxi with a painting.

JOANIE: Oh, yes. Ted. The gallery guy.

MAY: He was here?

JOANIE: He was looking at my work.

MAY: Was he looking at my work?

JOANIE: He wasn't.

MAY: Why did he have my picture?

JOANIE: *(Caught)* He didn't have anything of yours.

MAY: It looked like the one you took.

JOANIE: I threw that away.

MAY: It looked like that picture.

JOANIE: Oh. Oh, you're right. It was your canvas.
I figured why throw out a perfectly good canvas.
I painted over it. That's why I gave you a clean canvas.
To make up for it. For the one I painted over. The one
that was yours. It was my painting on your old canvas.

(MAY *knows it was her painting.*)

MAY: Did I ever see it?

JOANIE: No. No.

MAY: I'd like to see it.

JOANIE: Well. If it doesn't sell, it'll come back and you
can see it.

MAY: He's going to sell it?

JOANIE: He's showing it to some people. At his gallery.

MAY: He's going to show that picture at his gallery?
Downtown?

JOANIE: Yes. He'll probably show my work from now
on. A step up from the restaurant. Yes.

MAY: So—no more selling on the street for you.

JOANIE: I wasn't there to sell...I was there to remind
myself of the struggle. That's all I was doing.

MAY: Well. I can't wait to go downtown and see that
picture hanging in a gallery.

JOANIE: I don't...know that he's going to hang it. He
may just sell it. To a collector. Let me see what you're
working on. (*She looks and is taken aback.*) What is this?!
What are you doing now?!

MAY: All that talking we did about water. Made me
want to try it.

JOANIE: That's the face underwater?

MAY: Yes. It's the face. You can't really see it, though.
I'm sorry I put the water on top of it. Looks kind of sad,
doesn't she?

JOANIE: Very sad.

MAY: Because of the water, I think. Like she's drowned
or something.

JOANIE: ...And you got this effect how, exactly?

MAY: Oh—under water is deep—so I put a whole
bunch of layers on, then I wiped it with that stinky
stuff to make ripples. It's a technique I made up.

JOANIE: You made it up, you took paint and made it up,
you just made it up, you make up techniques now,
you patent them, your own special art forms, the May
Technique, not to be confused with the June, July,
or Joanie Techniques. Did you learn it in class, this
technique?

MAY: No.

JOANIE: Then it's not a technique.

MAY: Okay, it's not a technique, I don't care what
you call it.

JOANIE: "Wiped it with the stinky stuff —" God...

MAY: Don't be mad. I did the leaf, too. Look, here it is,
the leaf. I did what you said. I practiced leaf technique.
Don't be mad at me. I didn't mean to jump ahead.

JOANIE: What makes you think this is ahead?

MAY: It just seemed more advanced than a leaf. A face
under water seems more advanced than a leaf that is
not underwater.

JOANIE: Master the leaf before you call it baby work.

MAY: I'm not calling it anything. It's hard to paint a
leaf. The plumpiness is hard. The little arch in its back,

and how you capture that arch is with your light, right? how you make the light hit the leaf is how you make the plumpiness on the canvas. I couldn't have painted the cheek in the face except that I had painted the leaf first.

JOANIE: And now you shall paint the leaf properly. When you do that, you will see that a leaf is actually more advanced than a face under water.

MAY: *(Venturing some sarcasm)* Should I "throw it away?"

JOANIE: I'll throw it away. Let's see you make some progress with the anatomy of a leaf. Practice the leaf. I'll take this downstairs. To the dumpster.

MAY: *(Sarcasm.)* Yeah, maybe Ted's taxi hasn't left yet.

JOANIE: What?!

MAY: Okay, Ms Silver. Whatever you say, Ms Silver.

JOANIE: Don't use that tone on me. I can refund your money, and you're out the door. Is that what you want?

MAY: I want the lessons. I don't care what you do with my pictures.

JOANIE: ...Paint the leaf, please.

9

(The next morning. NICK at home)

(JOANIE enters.)

JOANIE: I was afraid you'd changed the locks.

NICK: Why would I do that?

JOANIE: It's standard operating procedure with a divorce.

NICK: Somebody you know getting a divorce?

JOANIE: ...I was afraid you'd have somebody over.

NICK: What, a woman?

JOANIE: It crossed my mind.

NICK: Then why didn't you call?

JOANIE: You are completely uncommunicative on the phone.

NICK: Are you moving back in, or what?

JOANIE: I miss you.

NICK: Well, that's a start.

JOANIE: Ted's showing my work—in his gallery.

NICK: Congratulations.

JOANIE: I'm thrilled, of course.

NICK: I guess you are.

JOANIE: It doesn't mean as much as I thought it would.

NICK: Oh?

JOANIE: Nobody to share it with.

NICK: All those artistic types. Your students.

JOANIE: See, that's the thing. None of them are going to be really happy for me. Any artist I tell, he's just going to be really sad that it isn't him. There isn't enough to go around. It makes everybody really jealous. So, I thought, isn't there anybody who would just be happy for me?

NICK: Good old Nick.

JOANIE: That's not exactly how I put it, when I thought of you.

NICK: What painting is it?

JOANIE: ...One of the new ones.

NICK: Great. I'll go down this afternoon and see it.

JOANIE: No. You don't have to.

NICK: Are you kidding? I want to.

JOANIE: No. You've seen it already.

NICK: You said it's new.

JOANIE: It's one you saw. You saw it. Wait until I paint one you haven't seen. Then we'll both go look at it. We'll wear sunglasses so nobody recognizes us.

NICK: It's a date.

JOANIE: It feels really good, Nick. It feels alive. My artistic juices are flowing...I miss you. I really miss you.

NICK: Yeah? We going to be boyfriend and girlfriend now?

JOANIE: Was that so bad?

NICK: Who can remember that long ago?

JOANIE: I remember our first dance. Your feet never moved, but your hands were all over me.

(JOANIE *and* NICK *kiss.*)

NICK: Thank you, Jesus...

JOANIE: Oh, Nick.

NICK: You're coming home.

JOANIE: I didn't say that.

NICK: I'll call Jake. He can go get your stuff from the studio.

JOANIE: Don't call Jake.

NICK: He knows how to drive the Titan.

JOANIE: I don't want him touching my stuff.

NICK: He won't take anything.

JOANIE: No, neither one of them. I don't want them in the studio. He'll take her with him. She mustn't go in the studio.

NICK: She's there all the time—

JOANIE: No, I'm not giving classes. That's all over.

NICK: What's going on?

JOANIE: Nothing. I can handle it.

NICK: Handle what?

JOANIE: I know about you, Nick. You'll overreact. You'll call out the big guns.

NICK: Overreact to what? *(A pause)* Tell me or I'm going to overreact.

JOANIE: I don't even know how to begin.

NICK: Just tell me.

JOANIE: She's stalking me. It's, it's completely wacky. I can't leave the studio at night—she's outside waiting. She's obsessed with me.

NICK: She admires you.

JOANIE: She shows up at the studio at all hours of the day and night. If I don't open the door, she stands outside my window.

NICK: I'll talk to Jake.

JOANIE: Half the time he's with her!

NICK: *(Disbelief)* Jake?

JOANIE: I looked out my window, and she was there, two o'clock in the morning. She was dressed just like me, I thought, I'm dreaming. They were both standing there, waiting for me to look outside—it was so creepy... I was scared. Me. Can you believe it?

NICK: Jake? Jake and May Carter?

JOANIE: I know. It's unbelievable. I think they want to be us. That's why he wants to work for you. She's copying my paintings. Not just my demonstrations, but the paintings that are mine—my face paintings. The first time I noticed, I thought it was some joke, she had completely copied it. She said, how do you like it? I said of course I like it, it's exactly like mine. She said, "It's nothing like yours. It's completely original—it's mine, it's mine." She screamed it, like an insane person. Screamed it. Can you believe it?

(And NICK *does not.)*

NICK: No.

JOANIE: ...I know, it's surreal. I had to go to the doctor. I thought I was going to have a heart attack—my heart races now. Look, I'm taking these pills. You know, maybe you should take care of it. Maybe it's too big for me to take care of.

NICK: *(From an emotional distance)* What do you have in mind?

JOANIE: I don't know—how should I know? Isn't that what you do? Take care of things?

NICK: You would like me to talk to May?

JOANIE: Talking isn't going to take care of it.

NICK: And this is why you've come here? For me to take care of May?

JOANIE: ...No, I came here because I miss you. You don't have to take care of anything, I'll take care of it myself—

NICK: How exactly do you plan on doing that?

JOANIE: I know how to take care of people...what? You think I haven't been paying attention for the last twenty years? I'll take care of May—

NICK: You will do nothing. *(Brief pause)* I will take care of it.

JOANIE: I can handle it myself.

NICK: Stop talking, Joan. *(A pause. He formulates the deal.)* I want you to move back in.

JOANIE: It's true—she's stalking me—

NICK: You move back in. I will take care of it. I will take care of this problem you have. This problem of someone "copying your work".

JOANIE: She is—!

NICK: Enough, Joan. I said. I will take care of it. And you will move back in.

JOANIE: *(Brief pause)* ...Alright.

NICK: And you will stay moved in. There will be no more separations. There will be no more talk of divorces.

JOANIE: And you'll—

NICK: I'll take care of it.

10

(That night. MAY *at her apartment)*

*(*MAY *is looking at a small painting.* JAKE *enters.)*

JAKE: You're not gonna believe this, May—

MAY: Look.

JAKE: Hey, who did that?

MAY: I got it. It finally came all at once.

JAKE: It's you.

MAY: No, it's my mother.

JAKE: She's beautiful.

MAY: Yeah.

JAKE: She looks just like you.

MAY: I know. All this time, I could have just looked in a mirror. What's on your nice shirt?

JAKE: I stopped at the garage.

MAY: And fixed an engine?

JAKE: They couldn't figure it out. It was a beautiful thing. You should have seen me. I was an engine PhD.

MAY: Oh, Jake. You should go back to the garage.

JAKE: Yeah. So. *(All smiles)* You ever heard of Kenosha?

MAY: Is that some kind of sausage?

JAKE: It's a city in Wisconsin.

MAY: I've heard of Wisconsin.

JAKE: We're going there.

MAY: For vacation?

JAKE: We're moving. *(Shows airline tickets)* Two tickets in two hours. There's a garage there I'm going to own.

MAY: How can you own a garage? We barely own shoes.

JAKE: It's a kind of witness protection.

MAY: ...Oh, my God, Jake—

JAKE: Witness protection in reverse.

(Brief pause)

MAY: I don't get it.

JAKE: Nick wants us to get lost. Forever.

MAY: What did you do—? Jake, what happened?

JAKE: We'll change our name. May, this is right. As soon as he said it I knew it was right, even though I'd never heard it before. Kenosha—sounds like Nebraska. It'll be easier for me to find my way around a town named Kenosha. In a garage. And you can get along any place. If you want to get a job, that's okay, too. Check, right? Check?

MAY: Check what? What are you saying?

JAKE: We'll lay low for a while. Don't worry, you can still paint— You still want to paint, don't you?

MAY: Paint? Jake, it's just a hobby—who cares?!

JAKE: You don't care about painting?

MAY: I don't care.

JAKE: Since when?

MAY: Since today. Since I painted Ma.

JAKE: Maybe you *should* take up something else.

MAY: Take up—? What? Like knitting—? What are you talking about?

JAKE: Knitting, sure, it's cold there. You could knit me sweaters. Let's go.

MAY: We're going *now*?

JAKE: Yeah, we gotta hurry. The car's outside.

MAY: What car? You got a car?

JAKE: Yeah, the Titan. I'm gonna leave it at the airport.

MAY: What should I take—? I don't know what to take.

JAKE: Take that. We'll hang it on a wall.

10

(JOANIE *and* NICK*'s place*)

(JOANIE *reads a magazine.* NICK *enters carrying a dress.*)

NICK: Time to go.

JOANIE: Where did you get that shirt?

NICK: Dress for Less.

JOANIE: You certainly do.

NICK: Come on. Let's go. Put this on.

JOANIE: What's that? I'm not going.

NICK: Yeah. Put it on. I picked it out special.

JOANIE: Why?

(*Pause*)

NICK: Why did I pick out a dress for you? Or why do
I want you to go out with me? I picked out a dress for
you because I was thinking about you when I passed
the store, and thought why doesn't Joanie wear
something like that for a change. Why I want you
to go out with me is you look very good on my arm;
it makes the guys happy to see you; and you are my
wife who the world should see having a great deal of
affection for me. Who goes with me when I invite her.
Who shoots me loving glances when others are looking.
Because that is her job. Which she does very well.
And without complaint. For which she is afforded
an enormous amount of luxury, respect, and freedom.
And whose problems she has with other artists get
taken care of. Put on the dress, Joan.

(JOANIE *tries to speak. No words come out.*)

END OF PLAY